inspired? get writing!

inspired?
get writing!

A fourth book of new poems and short stories inspired by the collection of the National Galleries of Scotland

National Galleries of Scotland

in association with the Scottish Poetry Library and the English-Speaking Union, Scotland

Published by the Trustees of the
National Galleries of Scotland 2013

Text © the authors

Images: p.11 © Martin Creed. Courtesy the artist and
Hauser & Wirth; p.13 © Damien Hirst and Science Ltd.
All rights reserved, DACS 2013; pp.15, 17 © Trustees
of the Paolozzi Foundation, Licensed by DACS 2013;
p.19 © Estate of Roy Lichtenstein / DACS 2013; p.33 ©
Callum Innes; p.35 © ARS, NY and DACS, London 2013;
p.37 © John Davies, Courtesy of Marlborough Fine Art;
p.41 *Two Men*, 1987–88, Freud, Lucian (1922–2011) /
Scottish National Gallery of Modern Art, Edinburgh, UK
/ The Bridgeman Art Library; pp.43, 45 © The Munch
Museum / The Munch – Ellingsen Group, BONO, Oslo /
DACS, London 2013; p.47 © Alison Watt; p.49 © Jannis
Kounellis; p.51 © Glenys Barton, Courtesy of Flowers
East, London; p.53 Courtesy of the artist, Luhring
Augustine, New York, and Gagosian Gallery; pp.55, 65 ©
Estate of Joan Eardley. All Rights Reserved, DACS 2013;
pp.57, 59, 63 © Succession Picasso / DACS, London 2013;
p.61 © ADAGP, Paris and DACS, London 2013.

Cover: Jannis Kounellis, *Bells*, 1993 (detail)
© Jannis Kounellis

Frontispiece: Alison Watt, *Sabine*, 2000 (detail)
© Alison Watt

ISBN 978 1 906270 64 3

Copy photography by Antonia Reeve and by John
McKenzie, except p.13 by Rick Jenkins and Donald
Thompson.

Designed by Dalrymple
Typeset in Verdigris and Modern no.20
Printed on Hello Matt 150gsm by Nicholson & Bass

National Galleries of Scotland is a charity registered
in Scotland no. SC003728

www.nationalgalleries.org

NATIONAL
GALLERIES
SCOTLAND

A NOTE ON THE CATEGORIES

The entries are accompanied by a note indicating
into which category they were entered:

CATEGORY A   under 12 years
CATEGORY B   12 – 14 years
CATEGORY C   15 – 18 years
CATEGORY D   adults' prose
CATEGORY E   adults' poetry

Foreword

Ekphrastic writing, or writing that has at its heart the description of a work of art, has a long tradition, and one which is celebrated by the *inspired? get writing!* creative writing competition. Writing about or from art not only helps us to understand art in new ways, but it is also an excellent inspiration for new writing.

We find more and more that one art form can help illuminate another, as poets are hired by galleries to help explain works of art to blind visitors, and artists explore the use of scent to help those who are deaf to experience new aspects of theatrical performances.

Since 2005, the National Galleries of Scotland, the English-Speaking Union Scotland and the Scottish Poetry Library have worked together to host this competition which encourages many people, including children, students, adults, people in various forms of care and others to access and engage with the National Galleries of Scotland's collection and to explore their own creativity through the use of the written word. The competition is not limited to Scottish shores and, over the past two years, we have been delighted to receive entries from Canada, Australia, Spain, Kuwait, Nepal and Hong Kong as well as throughout the UK. The presence of many of the Galleries' artworks online has now made the competition, and the collection generally, accessible to interested audiences the world over.

This year's publication includes the thirty top winning works from the 2012 and 2013 competitions. We are very grateful for generous support from the Gordon Fraser Charitable Trust, for the competition in general and the production of this fourth publication, from the Educational Institute of Scotland, for workshops for the winning schools, and to *The Scotsman*. Winners, friends, family and the general public will celebrate together at a reading and award ceremony held at the National Galleries of Scotland in Edinburgh.

We hope this competition will continue to open new routes of access both to the artworks held by the National Galleries of Scotland and to the various forms of writing that spring from creative engagement with art. We would like to thank the judges, sponsors and supporters who make this competition possible, and above all the writers and artists without whom we would not have so much beauty to revel in and be inspired by. We would also like to include in our thanks the organisers who work to maintain and grow the competition: Linda McClelland (National Galleries of Scotland), Suzanne Ensom (English-Speaking Union Scotland) and Lorna Irvine and Jennifer Williams (Scottish Poetry Library).

We hope that this volume, and the competition in coming years, will inspire people all over the world to look; and by looking may you learn, create and share your own individual, inspired and inspirational works of art in writing and any other forms that set your mind alight and your heart racing.

JOHN LEIGHTON
Director-General, National Galleries of Scotland

ROBYN MARSACK
Director, Scottish Poetry Library

BRIAN MONTEITH
Chairman, English-Speaking Union Scotland

'If you happened to be in the grounds of a certain art gallery in the middle of the night, and you peeked through a window of the place, you would see a massive shadow moving like a huge bat, flitting across the artwork on display. Vibrations would ripple through the ground and the occasional dull clang would echo from the gallery. And soon you would be scared off, running faster than a rabbit from a hunter in rabbit season.'

From I, *Statue* by Nathan Ezra-Jackson

Introduction

Several lifetimes ago I was a security guard at the Royal Scottish Academy gallery on the Mound. Money for jam – no uniform, and I was expected merely to stroll about the exhibition rooms keeping an eye on the visitors. If I saw someone attempting to photograph or to touch a painting, I moved into Jobsworth mode to spoil their fun. If I saw someone steal a painting, I became an action hero.

Not that I ever did. A few touchers, a few snappers, and that was about it. But what amazed me was that hardly a single visitor spent longer than thirty seconds in front of any given painting, if that. It was contemporary art, but they didn't give the paintings a chance, and they didn't give *themselves* a chance.

Which is one of the reasons that *inspired? get writing!* is such a wonderful idea. It is obvious from the work in this book that the writers spent a considerable time savouring their chosen painting, contemplating it, enjoying it, entering into the imaginative world of the artist and, most importantly, inviting the artist's creativity to touch and spark off their own.

Unless we see the world imaginatively, we hardly see it at all. Children are naturals, however. Spontaneous, trusting their imagination and not yet so over-educated as to believe that *thinking* is the be-and-end-all of life – for youngsters, seeing is a great adventure. In *I, Statue* – a playful take on Isaac Asimov's *I, Robot* – Nathan Ezra-Jackson shares his excitement with us by letting Eduardo Paolozzi's *Vulcan* become the story's narrator. I particularly enjoyed Eve McLachlan's *A Child's Fantasy*, where she describes bribing a lion with 'with fantasy / That I was growing too old to believe. / I will keep him lost in my dark woods'. Eve has created a truly poignant farewell to childhood innocence, a farewell weighted with genuine wisdom and sorrow.

Though older, Olga Wojtas and Darci Bysouth have each made a most original response to their chosen paintings. Olga made me laugh out loud with *The Procedure*, while Darci's very personal interpretation of Damien Hirst's *Chicken (from 'The Last Supper')* is deeply moving and without a trace of sentimentality. *Black and White*, by Peter Ratter, is a quite exceptional piece of work. It manages to convey Goya's image of horror with a fine sensitivity that transcends the accomplished formality of the verse. His poem is a miniature masterpiece.

Most of the poems and stories in this book stand by themselves, without reference to the paintings that suggested them. The translation from canvas to word has been complete and *inspired*. From eleven-year-old Ryan Cummins's deeply felt portrait of his new head teacher whose heart is 'as hard and cold as stone, / It was forged by the devil…' and Emma Wright's delightful flight of fancy, to the up-and-coming Iain Matheson's laconic brilliance and the artistic maturity of Ian McDonough, there is an extraordinary wealth of new and exciting work to be found in this volume.

Perhaps what you are about to read here will inspire you in turn – at the very least, to linger for much longer than usual in front of the paintings that you enjoy.

RON BUTLIN
Edinburgh Makar

Our Jar of Fireflies

by EMMA WRIGHT

If we walked to an airport – together, not apart
and climbed into one of the jumbo jets
(the ones with the bright lights
that blink so safely in the dark)
and let the pilot pull us into the cosmopolitan oblivion –
(the soft part of the clouds, in between the sun and the stars)

we'd climb out, and let the plane dip us down
so we reach the pillows the clouds lace out for us
and we'd be able to watch the city lights illuminate our toes –
like tiny fireflies patterned against the jumbo jet
shining when we need to understand
that everything is going to be alright

together, always together, we would watch the city lights fade
just out of reach from our fingertips –
just out of reach for us to bottle up and keep
safe inside our jumbo jet, our jar full of fireflies

and we'd stay outside on the clouds for a while,
pretending to catch the slowly fading lights in the gaps of our fingers
until the city lights went damp and dull beneath our feet
and we could no longer see the clouds we sit on
or each other's faces

but then we'd see the flickering lights reappear below us,
lighting up a message you could only see from the clouds
and the lights would let us know again
that everything will be alright.

[CATEGORY B]

statues and works of art, and humans, if this does not conflict with any of the previous laws.

I thought about what I should do. If I made the statue wouldn't that risk revealing that I was a living being, breaking the First Law? But I went ahead and built it anyway to show gratitude towards my creator for making me. The next morning Paolozzi found the statue. Just as I was taken away. So he got all the glory and the money when I actually did all the work. So unfair. But then what would I have done with the money anyway?

The next thing I knew I was bundled into a large white lorry and into darkness. The ride was long, bumpy and terrifying. Where was I going next? What was going on? I couldn't move. The men had tied me to a massive board of wood with strong metal cord. I lay down the whole journey. After what seemed like forever, I at last arrived here, the Scottish National Gallery of Modern Art Two (that's a bit of a mouthful, isn't it?), one of the only homes I've ever had.

Now, after my period of reflection, I asked myself the question again. *Am I art?* Yes. And it didn't seem so freaky anymore because now I know that anything could be art.

Even you.

[CATEGORY A]

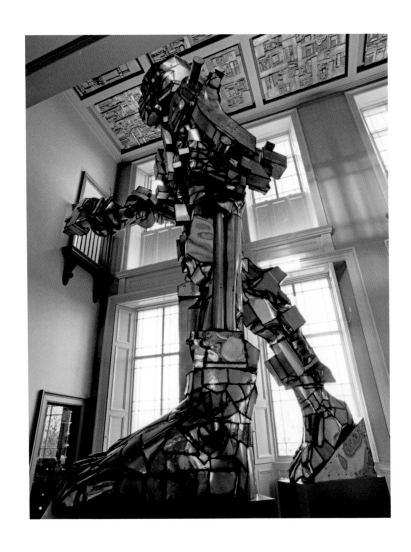

EDUARDO PAOLOZZI
Vulcan, 1998–9
GMA 4285 · commissioned 1999 (with aid from the Patrons of the
National Galleries of Scotland)

15

Cleish Panels

by DAN SPENCER

it's falling, it's made of shields and chest plates, and i build against it, i hammer, i tong, i torch, bring props, bring spears, i'm slow on my joisted leg, but hold, bring spears, lodge another spear in place, more spears, the sky is made of walls, they're falling

and it's all i can do, i'm a wreck on my feet, i'm a wreck on my legs, but i pile, i joist, i shore myself against it, a desert but i keep working, one foot then the other, build barricades, bring stones, bring spears, bring rubble, work, wreck, work, go on working

weld another panel into place, it's falling, any moment, a wreck, and a small figure, nothing, a spark, working, working, dreaming of a wife, under the sky, it's cornflower-grey, and as big as a ship, it's made of cranes, the sky, it's made of lakes, islands, rivers, cables

a boulder, a world, a city, lemon-grey, and streets, avenues, plazas, forums, colonnades, and blocks and blocks and blocks, and great public works, so how to stand against it? and why? who for? a lonely job, and endless, but you shore yourself, even as it falls

because it will, it is, it's falling, even as it rises, watch it falling, slowly, heavily, feather-grey, it's made of angles and circles, and cogs, from here i'm looking down on it, encompassing it, drawing a perfect circle, it's made of puzzles, formulas, codes

bring ladders, bring ropes, watch closely, watch it changing, add some colour, add some god-grey to the mix, there's a story there, it's figurative, it's a man, it comes down to a man, in the end, a great weak man, a lonely man, a great man reaching

even as it falls, a boulder, my head's a boulder and i'm falling, i'm turning over, even as i, but hold, dig the heels in, one foot then the other, why? don't ask why, but why? it's made of day on day on day, of working, forgetting, working, dreaming of you, dreaming

vulcan, ozymandias, noah, atlas, day after day, in the valleys and plains and terraced hills, like my father taught me, working, under a dawn sky, dreaming, under green-grey skies, rearranging, newton, michelangelo, sisyphus, abel, again and again, it goes on, i go on

16

[CATEGORY E]

EDUARDO PAOLOZZI
Detail from *Vulcan*, 1998–9
GMA 4285 · commissioned 1999
(with aid from the Patrons of the
National Galleries of Scotland)

Detail from *Cleish Castle
Ceiling Panel*, 1971–3
GML 859 – GML 867 · on loan
from the City of Edinburgh
Council's Museums and Galleries

Smoulder for a Dollar

by EVIE CLEPHAN

Well that's that. I've made up my mind to do it. I've done some wild things in the past that I'm not exactly proud of, but if I'm gonna do anything – well anything crazy I guess – it would be for her. Crazy, crazy beautiful that's what she is and I can't let her go. It's not even about the money anymore, ha! Well I'm not going to lie. Having a dollar or two ain't gonna be a bad thing. Sure we'll get her that diner of hers set up, but I'm thinkin' I might just go and get me a new car. It's not like this one's gonna be much good, not after today.

'You're sure about this hun?' I had to be certain, about this – about us.

She squeezed my thigh in response – my stomach was doing butterflies at her touch – whilst mouthing the word, 'Yes'. Her mouth was perfect, pink lips pouted to perfection and those long eyelashes… Boy I couldn't resist. I knew they were false like the pearls at her ears, like the blond of her hair; but there was nothing false about our love.

This was out of control and if it wasn't for the clown on the back seat of my car, we'd be sorted…

Why did I marry him? thought Cora. I should have never listened to my mother. 'He's steady,' she told me, 'He's going places.' What a joke. Four years together and he is never at home. 'Late bookings tonight,' or 'Playing cards with the boys after the restaurant closes.'

I'm not stupid. I've seen the looks, the looks he gives those waitresses. The drinking was the last straw. People tell me it's an occupational hazard of being a restaurant owner, but you can't tell me drinking that amount on a daily basis is normal. Brad might not be wealthy but he doesn't touch the bottle. He notices me, treats me well – with respect. He'll do anything for me, my tall dark and handsome guy. He'll do anything for me – even murder.

'We have to do it hun, it's the only way,' Brad whispered.

My attention was diverted to the slob on the back seat singing noisily. What an embarrassment – too drunk to stay in his own restaurant.

'We have to do it,' I whispered back, 'Tonight.'

He looks at me with those smouldering eyes. I cannot resist. I am all his.

'CUT!'

The director's instruction ended the scene and all hell broke loose on set.

'Lana, darling! How many times do I need to tell you – you're in love with Brad. Show it more, less of the cold fish, I've seen more passion at a zoo than between you two chimps.'

Lana rebutted furiously, 'Tay, it's the lights not me. I'm a professional smoulderer and I know for a fact that the lights are not catching the shadow of my face properly. As for you Dan, you must clean your teeth, or at least suck a mint before I even start to consider kissing you. And could you have not chosen a better tie, without a stain on it?'

That was it. Dan, the actor playing Brad, interjected while she paused for breath. 'Don't get started on me dear. That coat makes you look cheap. Brad would never date someone like you!'

At this point Chuck – who was playing the role of the husband – had had enough. 'Whoah! You pair of peacock preening prima donnas, steady on now. Get over here Tay, we need to talk money. I refuse to carry on with this pair of idiots. I need a pay rise if you want this picture finished.'

Tay Garnett, the director, threw up his arms in exasperation. He stormed to the back of the set, sat down on his chair and beckoned the assistant director over. 'Get Chuck's agent on the phone, and for heaven's sake make sure Dan's sober.' The sound of heels indignantly stomping off across the room drew his eyes back towards the set where Lana had indeed started to follow Chuck out of the building.

'On second thoughts, make sure you get Lana some flowers as well, nice ones mind, but not too expensive. You got that?'

'Yes sir, right away.' The assistant director hurried off.

'Little idiots,' muttered Tay fondly. He smiled and put out his hand to some ditzy wannabe who could place his cigars and lighter in it. Love and planned murder turned to diva drama and all with great expense, just another normal day in Hollywood.

ROY LICHTENSTEIN
In the Car, 1963
GMA 2133 · purchased 1980

A Child's Fantasy

by EVE MCLACHLAN

I caught a lion yesterday.
He came to me, you see. Not the other way around.
I bribed him with innocence and pale dreams
A grandmother's jacket, sewn with fantasy
That I was growing too old to believe.
I will keep him lost in my own dark woods –
An inverted fairy tale –
His head too fine to mount upon a wall.

[CATEGORY C]

The Bell Rock Enigma

by ELEANOR KIRKLAND

'Hello,' croaked a hoarse voice at the other end of the line. 'Is that Off-shore Electrics?'

'It is, how can we help you?' the bored receptionist replied.

'My name is William Mallord and I am the lighthouse keeper on Bell Rock. Can you please send out an electrician to examine the main beacon? I am very concerned that it is losing power and intensity, and it must be dealt with before the winter storms begin.'

'Of course Sir…'

'Oh, and send a kind, strong, good hearted young man please.'

That was the end of the call. Violet Collins sat at her desk in her tiny office, and thought to herself, 'Nobody is ever going to sign up for such a risky job. Who'd want to go to Bell Rock of all places? Who knows how long you could be stuck there!' Still thinking, she went off to put up a notice about the job. She was not surprised a week later, when she found herself replacing it, at triple the pay, as no-one had shown any interest.

As he read it, Antony Harrison smiled with relief. He really needed money to buy an engagement ring for his girlfriend, Michelle. He was also going to need a lot of courage to propose to her, but he would worry about that later. Quickly, he signed up for the job and two days later he was on a boat, lurching his way towards the treacherous Bell Rock.

William Mallord was eighty years old and a sober looking fellow. His face was very pale, his eyes bloodshot and his spindly limbs stiff and cold. He was so thin and frail you could see almost every vein and feel just about every bone in his body. His wispy hair was the colour of sea froth, and his irregular breathing rattled and rasped like the stormy March winds. He was like an old, battered ship which had experienced many journeys and known many secrets, but had seen better days.

Antony arrived very late at night and as the boat sped off into the mist, he felt very alone, and a little nervous. After a short conversation with the old man, he went to bed, or rather, he curled up on a small, dilapidated sofa, gripping a thin blanket as tightly as his numb fingers allowed. When he finally dozed off, he dreamt of Michelle, of them getting married, having children and growing old together; his whole life seemed to flash before his very eyes. He woke suddenly, shivering with cold. 'How does the old man not catch pneumonia?!' he thought to himself. As the pale dawn light crept above the horizon, he got his first chance to survey the room properly. It was rather bare, with only the little sofa and an old chair in one corner, a table set for breakfast and a small table with a telephone on it and an ancient radio. There were also two doors leading out of the room; he presumed that one led to Mr Mallord's bedroom and the other to the light beacon and electrical systems. The walls were a gentle yellow, the ceiling white. Everything was old and tattered; the paint was flaking and all of the materials were faded and threadbare. There weren't even any curtains at the large, drafty window, through which he could see a grey, restless sea and great dark clouds gathering in the sky; there would probably be a storm later. At breakfast he asked Mr Mallord why he stayed on this desolate island. His reply left Antony feeling slightly uneasy and a little sad. 'It was my destiny to live here, I couldn't possibly leave.'

The old man sank down into his chair. He looked tired and ill and as he quietly drifted off to sleep, Antony carefully ascended the steep, spiralling stone steps to take a look at the light. The old man was right, it was strangely opaque. He embarked on a methodical check of the lamps, lenses, mirrors, master switches and control boards. After a long and diligent search he slumped down against the curved wall, tired and confused.

Outside, a dense fog had descended and the ominous rumble of thunder rolled across the sky. The sea was like a ravenous beast, ready to engulf and devour any passing ships. As he gazed, mesmerised by the towering waves crashing onto the jagged rocks below, he wondered when on earth he would get back to the warmth and familiarity of home.

Downstairs, Mr Mallord was awake again. Antony entered, brows furrowed with frustration. 'Mr Mallord, I've just been upstairs to take a look at the light and you were right, it's definitely not as strong as it should be. However, what is puzzling me is that I couldn't find any problem with the power source. Is there something that I am missing, a transformer perhaps?'

William gave a soft chuckle. 'Haven't you realised? It's right in front of you.'

'Mr Mallard, I don't quite understand…'

'You understand perfectly, you just don't want to accept the truth.'

Those were his last words. Antony stared, paralysed with horror as the exhausted body fell limp. For a few moments, the room seemed frozen in time. The deafening silence was suddenly shattered by the desolate groan of a ship's foghorn.

Antony felt as if his heart would burst out of his chest. Salty tears crashed down his ghostly face. He knew that only he could save the people on that ship but that to do so, he would have to live a long and solitary life. He would never marry Michelle and never have children. He would live and die alone.

The horn sounded again, much closer this time. Antony made his decision.

[CATEGORY A]

JOSEPH MALLORD WILLIAM TURNER
Bell Rock Lighthouse, 1819

D 5181 A · purchased by Private Treaty Sale 1989 with the aid of funds from the National Heritage Memorial Fund and the Pilgrim Trust

Black and White

by PETER RATTER

If you think you understand pain, then try
this: a world awash with black blood, white
widows, where my friends are canvasses. Cry
for them, pray for them, and their fading fight.

Then a sharp shot, a crimson explosion.
How is this from your perspective? My boots
are soaked. A blindfolded corpse, a gun.
You're here to adjust my easel. One shoots;

another creation, but so much paint spilled;
it's a new masterpiece shelved, and I'm still
painting, daubing what the audience willed.
I tell you my friend, this is how men kill.

[CATEGORY C]

FRANCISCO DE GOYA Y LUCIENTES
Y no hai remedio (And there is no help),
plate 15 of *The Disasters of War*, 1809–14
GOYA.11 · purchased 1967

Y no hai remedio.

Sweet as Sugar

by MARGARET SESSA-HAWKINS

This was the month Iain didn't write. He wrote as often as he could, and though the letters were sporadic it had never been more than two weeks between them. And now there was nothing.

Though she didn't say anything about it, Mary was worried. Angela – who had known Mary since childhood – could see. Mary was always so genuinely happy, even through these past years. Now though, even as she smiled and laughed, and talked the same as she always had, some light in her eyes had dimmed.

Iain and Mary had been dating since the end of school. They had gotten engaged just before the war broke out. It was when he left that Angela had suggested they get jobs. Most girls then were volunteering as nurses, but they had gotten the job in the sugar factory because it was nearby, and had spent the last three years spreading shovelfuls of sugar over the floor to air it out.

For the most part it had kept them occupied, and happy. But now Mary – who was supposed to be airing the sugar – was spreading it around on the floor in the same manner as a child spreads vegetables it doesn't want to eat around its plate.

'Mary,' called out Angela, and her friend looked up. Angela carefully considered what she would say next, how she would phrase it. 'Have you ever thought, I meant not like you would do it or anything, because of course you wouldn't, but have you ever just thought…'

They talked as they worked together, quickly piling shovelfuls of sugar higher and higher. It seemed to Angela that Mary's tongue was looser, that her eyes held the kindling of a spark they hadn't held before. They had only been working for fifteen minutes, however, before Doris walked by.

If Doris was not universally reviled, it was only because the universe was infinite. She was strict, and sour, and as she stared at the small progress Angela and Mary had so far made, the edges of her lips sank down, and Angela knew they were through.

'Doris,' Angela's head whipped around as she heard Mary speak. 'Have you ever thought, not that you would ever do it, because of course you wouldn't, not in a million years, but have you ever just thought…'

And Doris picked up a shovel.

They had been working steadily for quite a while before a group of workers caught them. Oblivious of the time, they were caught unawares as the girls passed them on the way downstairs for lunch. Off-guard, the girls just stood, gaping at Doris, Angela and Mary's handiwork. For a few brief moments, there was silence. It was Doris who broke it.

'Oh come on you lot,' she said roughly. 'You know you've thought about it.'

And suddenly, everyone had a shovel.

By the end of the hour, the mountain of sugar was almost to the ceiling. At this point they had used up all the sugar on the floor, and had been running all over the factory, bringing in the grains from other rooms, leaving a trail of sweet crumbs behind them on the floor, a cheer going up as each bit was added to the pile.

'I think that's about it,' said Angela finally, looking up at the gigantic white mound.

'All right then,' said one of the workers. 'Who's first?'

'Mary is,' said Angela, just as Mary cut in with 'Angela'.

But in the end it was Mary who slipped and slid and finally managed to clamber her way up to the top of the pile. She sat on the very apex of the mountain, folded her skirt daintily between her legs, lifted her heels up, and pushed off.

She was silent as she slid down the pile, and Angela was fearful, having expected her to shout out in delight. When Mary reached the bottom she wiped her sleeve across her face, and Angela saw they were glittering. Then Mary's face broke out into a grin and she turned to the other girls.

'You. Must. Try that.' She declared. So one by one, they did. Some screamed and shouted, others laughed, and some, like Mary, were silent.

GEORGE P. LEWIS

Spreading Refined Sugar Before Bagging, Glebe Sugar Refinery, Greenock, 1918/2004

PGP 310.11 · commissioned by the Gallery in 2004 from negatives held in the Imperial War Museum

Angela was one of the last to go. It was a strange feeling, sitting on top of the mound. It was, in fact, what everyone had thought of. It was the one thing you could not do. But now you were living in a world where people ordered your friends and family to far-away places, working in a factory when every day of your life for the past three years you had been made to show your pockets and shake out your dress. So you made a huge pile of sugar. So you sat on top of it. So you slid down.

And as you slid you thought of your brother, who had been one of the first to go, and one of the first who never came back. You thought about chocolate and how much you ached to eat just one simple square. You thought about gardening with your mother, and running home from school with Mary, and sitting down to eat together, as a family.

She reached the bottom almost crying but feeling strangely light. It seemed that crazy ideas engendered themselves because sliding down she had been struck by another. Grabbing a shovel she cut ahead of the line shouting, 'Make way, make way, woman with a shovel!' And dragging the shovel, she made the laborious climb up to the top.

In the moment before she jumped on the shovel she

thought, very clearly, 'This is how I will die.' Then she was on the shovel, riding down the mountain, the handle firmly in her hands, and then she was at the bottom, laughing like a lunatic, several girls already in front of her, clamouring for the shovel so they could give it a try.

They left that day just like any other, having spread the sugar across the floor, and turning their pockets out and shaking their skirts as they walked out the door. But she remembered. Well after the war had ended and beyond the point where life had moved on.

She remembered it at odd moments, when she felt that life had somehow jumped the tracks, and then continued running down a completely new path. That – though she loved them dearly – she had married someone who had not been intended for her, had given birth to children that weren't quite hers, and she now moved in strange circles.

They – none of them – understood, so she never even tried to tell the story. But whenever she and Mary had tea, she couldn't help, as she dropped in the tiny cubes, betraying a small smile.

I Stood as a Crofter …

by JENNY MCGUIRE

I stood as a crofter.
I wept as a boy.
I embraced mah Faither as a son.

Nae-buddy spoke,
Juist stood 'n' watched,
As th' fire licked lik' a moggie at oor wee hoose.

Women crying,
Men shouting.
Smoke whirling 'n' making me cough.

I kent what wis cumin,
Only didnae want to face it.
I turned around and could see Mither's face redden.

'Laddies,' declared mah Mither,
Tears streaming doon her coupon,
'We're gaun tae Canada!'

Waiting at th' quayside,
Watching time gang by.
I did' ney see mither bolt away.

So aff gaed we,
In th' blink o an eye.
Proud stow-aways oan a Glescae steamer.

Ah jump tae attention,
As mah teacher reads a line.
She's reading that same story.

'Eliza laughs once more.
Her family are together again.'
Then mah teacher says triumphantly, *'The End!'*

I kin shut th' book oan Eliza's story,
But ah cannae shut it oan mine.
I still have pages of my story unwritten.

[CATEGORY A]

JEAN-BAPTISTE GREUZE

A Boy with a Lesson-book

NG 436 · bequest of Lady Murray of Henderland 1861

The Full Moon

by ISABELLA BOYD

He appeared that busy day at the harbour. The inn was full of richly dressed merchants who had just disembarked from a grand ship called the *Queen Beth*. He was a sad and sorry looking man wearing a torn blue coat and worn-out hose. His black hair fell onto his shoulders in long straggly strands and he walked with a slight limp. His face was strewn with cuts and bruises and his eyes were bloodshot with dark baggy rings beneath them. You could tell from a distance that he had come from the sea. He had arrived at our inn with nothing more than a small wooden box as luggage and demanded a room, not telling us for how many nights he would be lodging.

All he did day in and day out was sit in the corner of the bar and drink bottles of rum to his heart's content. He never spoke to anyone or told anyone his name but just sat raising his hand when he wanted another bottle. So that was how it was for a week or so. The merchants kept flooding in and our strange guest remained.

It was one day while I was walking upstairs to my room, when coming from the strange sea captain's room I heard a groaning like I'd never heard before. My first instinct was to go in and check on him but knowing his solitary nature I thought otherwise. My mind was made up when I heard a ghastly groan that made my stomach turn in fear. I opened the door quickly and was faced with a scene no boy of my age would ever want to witness. On the bed, tossing and turning, clutching at his side was the old sea captain. The bed sheets once green were now a horrid blood red. I ran to his side immediately. 'Sir, sir can I help you, are you all right?' I said frantically, kneeling down beside his bed. 'Can I call a doctor?' I cried, desperate to help.

The captain turned to face me. I could see his whole face, pasty white with loss of blood. His eyes were wide and owl-like staring into mine so helplessly. I could hear his quick breathing as he tried to hang onto life. 'No, a doctor wouldnae get here in time,' he whispered so faintly I had to lean closer to hear. 'But boy!' he continued urgently, 'do one thing for me

will you and look under my bed and bring out what you find!'

I can't explain what my thoughts were at this point. My head swam and my heart beat so quickly that I could feel it pounding in my chest so I didn't delay. I reached under the bed and, as I did so, felt something cool against my hot sweaty palm. I glanced up at the captain whose strength I could see was draining rapidly. So, as quickly as possible, I pulled out the object which I found beneath the bed. I literally stopped and stared, totally stupefied, for what I was holding in the palm of my hand was a perfectly round, sparkling diamond!

'There she is,' the captain sighed in awe, *'The Full Moon!'*

'The Full Moon,' I whispered back, totally mesmerised by the stunning object which I beheld.

'Boy, you must guard this with your life like I've done with mine!' he uttered urgently. 'Don't let anyone take this from you, do you understand?' I nodded slowly. His words were hardly audible now. I knew his time was nearly up. So I watched as the captain fell limply onto his pillows, his face expressionless, his body lifeless.

The inn was in total chaos over the next few days. I told my parents everything, everything apart from *The Full Moon*, which I kept hidden in my room. I couldn't help feeling that it was the reason that the captain was murdered. I wanted to know more about this precious diamond, especially how much it was worth. So on the first day that the inn was quiet I went out into the bustling streets of the town, sprinted past the usually tempting market stalls and ran straight into the jeweller's shop. A bald bespectacled man looked at me rather inquisitively from behind a pair of round horn-rimmed glasses.

'What can I do for you son?' he asked politely.

'Please can you tell me how much this is worth?' I said proudly as I placed *The Full Moon* on the table.

'Certainly,' the man replied, taking out a loupe from his jacket pocket to inspect it for some moments. Finally the jeweller looked up and said, 'I'm afraid son, this jewel you've

got here is as good as fake it is. Where did you get it from?'

'What?' I said dismayed, 'No it can't be!' With that, I snatched up *The Full Moon* and replaced it with a sixpence then rushed out of the door bewildered into the street. I felt I'd been made such a fool of. An old sea dog's last trick and I'd fallen for it. I felt so annoyed. How could I have thought that this 'diamond' was worth anything?

By this time I was back at the inn. I ran straight up to my room and stood there annoyed, stunned, staring at the 'diamond'. Suddenly in a sudden frantic passion for revenge I hurled *The Full Moon* at the floor. I heard it shatter into a million tiny shards on the ground at my feet. After some moments of standing stubbornly there I glanced down at the damage. Among the tiny glittering shards I saw a rolled up bit of parchment. It was stained and old. It was torn and burned at the edges and as I knelt to pick it up I could feel how delicate it was. I slowly unrolled it and I could see elegant script written in black ink. It was a map with location coordinates and a large 'X marks the spot' in the middle of a neatly drawn island saying '*There be Treasure*'. So I hadn't been fooled. *The Full Moon* was just a decoy. This map was the real thing. I felt so much power as I beheld this Treasure Map. I would guard it with my life.

[CATEGORY A]

GEORGE WASHINGTON WILSON
View in Leith Docks, 1860s
PGP R 206 · gift of Mrs Riddell in memory of Peter Fletcher Riddell, 1985

Six Identified Forms

by JAMES GAO

Darkness
    at a corn field;
six farmers pick their way through husks
brought down by the storm. Their wives,
roused by the thunder, standing by the now
coldest door of their homes, fumble out gold torches;
without *any* certainty that the batteries are not dead.

        The night is not dead,
        but now it is night,
        the wind declines, abates, subsides
and falls. With rolling oils of cloud cover,
the men are drawn out like wicks
past the moon. One by one they look in
the dark to see the stars wash
themselves clean of weather; and – together –
align, as the constellation of a limping dog,
once lost – now homeward bound.

        One farmer kneels
        down: sees something
shiny, of interest, on the floor of the field.
He goes to pick it up, and everything else stops.
His companions stop. With no word said,
nor any need expressed, six matches bend on strike,
burning like the long stalks that blink one by one,
            slowly. And by one and one more
            there is a dog bark,
that does nothing to disturb the hushed crops.
His companions wait. It is a timeless night,
that'll turn day soon: all forms of life know this.

[CATEGORY C]

CALLUM INNES
Six Identified Forms, 1992
GMA 3670 · purchased (Knapping Fund) 1993

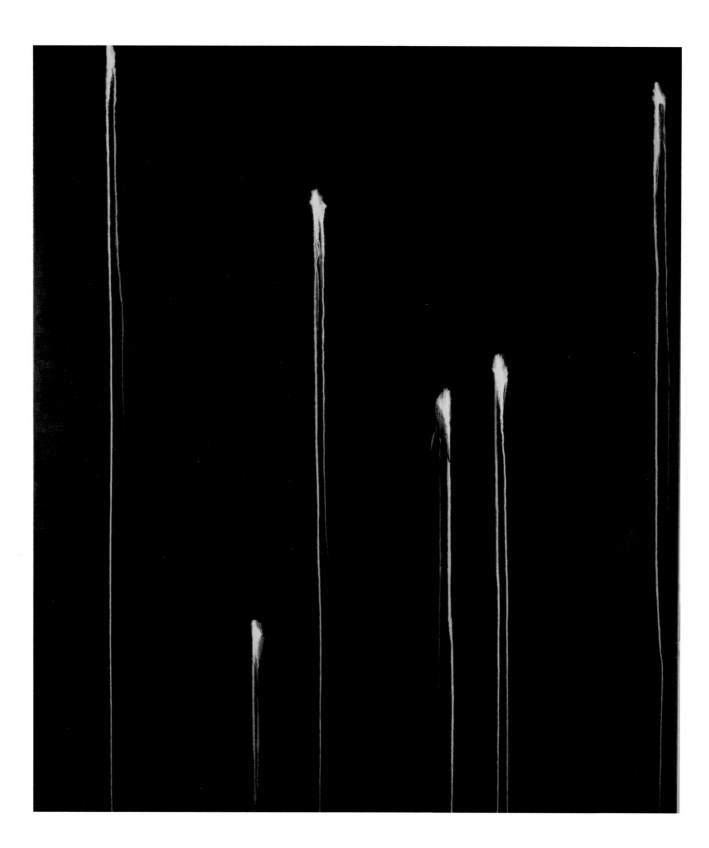

The Rainbow-Snake

by NATHAN EZRA-JACKSON

Zem wriggled through the sky, effulgence emitting from her abdomen, spinning a rainbow out of light like a spider would a web. The rain lashed over her vividly-coloured skin but the sun shone through the curtains of dreary drizzle, calling her. She needed to do her work. A rainbow was required and she had to make it. As she spun the light, she tried to keep herself from twitching or recoiling from the glare. It rained a lot on her assigned town, Edinburgh. Sun was rare. So when there were conditions for a rainbow (which was not very often) she would be ready in the wings. Every time.

Other rainbow-snakes, like the ones in the tropics where there were rainbows every day, would lazily flourish a barely-qualifying tatty rainbow and flutter back to their nest, as they were so common.

Zem savoured each flight like it was her last, drawing in the precious energy which gave her the power to produce rainbows. She continued wriggling along, weaving her rainbow, when she glimpsed a multi-coloured, curvy-shaped thing through a window of a large house. *It could be another rainbow-snake! Captured!*

Her curiosity piqued, she hurried the rest of her work then met up with a few leprechauns burying their crock of gold in the cloud at the end of her freshly-formed rainbow.

It was Gary and Crick.

'Yo, Zemmy,' called Crick, resting his shovel against the cloud.

'How ya doin'?' asked Gary.

Zem slowed down as she approached them, the rain and cold Scottish wind battering her. 'In a rush,' she panted.

'What's the hurry?' asked Crick. 'Normally, after a job you're off like a bullet to your nest. Us leprechauns ain't as lucky as you. Minin' for gold at the end of the rainbow all the time.'

'Then what do we get to do with the gold?' snorted Gary. 'Fill a crock with the stuff, and leave it there to dissolve into vapour: the humans are too dumb to ever even *look* at the end of the rainbow. The only payment we get is the gold-dust that's left over.'

'I think I've spotted another rainbow-snake,' said Zem urgently, wanting to evade their rant. 'In a human habitat! Bye!'

And with that, she flapped her sky-fin and shot off. As she dipped to street-level, her hide shimmered and turned mirror-like, reflecting her surroundings so to just a close observer she looked like a slight haze in the air.

Even if there had been a close observer, the downpour shielded that haze. Zem whisked over a strange garden and honed in on the building she'd glimpsed the multi-coloured squiggle in. She hovered in front of the window and peered in. And gasped with horror. A rainbow-snake was on the wall. It was mounted and stretched so it was taut all around the room! There was a little sign in human language which said something like *Sol LeWitt Wall Drawing* and then loads of other stuff. She was shocked at how ignorant the humans walking about the room were. They were staring at the body of a rainbow-snake!

Zem instinctively acted. She smashed through the window and hissed out a string of snake-speak to the poor snake nailed to the wall.

'Are you alright!? Can you hear me!?'

People were screaming and running away from the shards of glass.

The snake didn't reply. She shot onto the wall, hissing, trying to reassure the poor thing. And then Zem realised that it WASN'T a snake, it was a drawing. So she soared through the room, still invisible, towards the window. But there was a human there, and he smashed a little red box on the wall. Immediately a horrible ringing sound screamed through the building. Zem was terrified and bolted away from the shattered window. The shrill sound kept on going. Her invisibility slipped. She heard the hammer of running feet and realised that she needed to hide. But there was nowhere to hide and

her invisibility was temporarily gone due to fright.

The footsteps were getting closer and closer.

Zem suddenly had an idea. She could blend into the wall-drawing! She flattened herself against the coloured work of art painted onto the wall, and curved her body over it, closing her eyes. To a casual passer-by, she was completely blended in to the picture.

Some security guards and staff came blundering into the room and started speaking into their radios. Soon, a load of police came piling into the room. Zem was terrified and the police started hunting around with their sniffer dogs, fingerprint scanners and DNA scanners. Zem flattened herself to the painting and formulated a plan. She turned herself red and hooped herself around a sniffer-dog's red

collar. The dog shook its neck violently and barked.

'What's wrong, Max?' asked a policemen, leaning down to the dog.

At this point, Zem rocketed off the dog's neck and out into the rain again, where the rainbow she had spun was already beginning to fade.

[CATEGORY A]

SOL LEWITT
Wall Drawing #1136, 2004
AR00165 · Artist Rooms National Galleries of Scotland and Tate. Acquired jointly through The d'Offay Donation with assistance from the National Heritage Memorial Fund and the Art Fund 2008

35

The Doctor

by CAT DEAN

The morning after the Museum of London was looted, I was late. I arrived sweating and out of breath but before Elliot.

'Divination in twenty minutes!' he shouted as he came in, depositing a wire cage on my desk. A gnarled red claw poked out and scratched at my keyboard.

Six months ago I would have been skeptical about this method of forecasting the markets but that was before the riots, before Black July and before the heads on spikes all over Canary Wharf.

'Come in for a pow-wow,' Elliot murmured to me, his hand resting on the edge of my desk.

I picked up my dandelion latte, some herbal crap they're selling as coffee these days, and followed Elliot into his office.

He sat down and picked a silky white feather off his pinstriped sleeve, his fingers curved into tweezers. He looked at me for a moment and then leant forward.

'H R called about the Decimation Scheme.'

'Great,' I said. I thought of Crawford's shiny black shoes tap-dancing in mid-air, his dick tentpoling his Jack Soni pinstripes, the urine blooming darkly over his crotch. The Olympic Stadium vibrating with the roar of eighty thousand people. The scent of sweat and burgers in the air.

'Your name came up.'

'Fantastic,' I said.

'Obviously Rosemary would benefit.'

I nodded. I looked outside and watched the ravens hopping along the heads from Lehmann, Goldman, Deutshe, R B S. Why wasn't Elliot down there with his mates? He hadn't even been branded.

'I hear they've appointed a new hangman. Ex-teacher. Thorough chap, apparently. Think about it, it's a good deal.'

Outside, a raven had stuck its beak into an empty eye socket and was poking about. Morgan Stanley or Merrill? Hard to tell now.

When I looked back at him, Elliot was wagging his finger at me in mock reprimand, saying, 'Glass half-full, Dougie, glass half-full!'

JOHN DAVIES
For the Last Time, 1970–2
GMA 3450 · purchased 1989

All the way through Divination, I was thinking about the Decimation Scheme. In many ways, Elliot was right, of course. A pension for dependents. Relocation costs. Prayers for the soul by professional mourners. A bonus for the sale of body parts. However, it was the permanent removal of names from the Register which mattered most; everyone agreed on that.

Climbing back up the stairs after Social Rehab, I was thinking of Rosie's face when I told her she could lose the armband. She and the boys would move somewhere, start afresh. York? Edinburgh?

I pushed on the office door and teetered on the edge of nothingness: instead of the clutter of desks, screens, chairs and pastel-coloured shirts, a grey sea of floor tiles stretched out in front of me. Square columns sprouted from the floors and cables sprung from the walls like weeds. I must have come up an extra flight. In the middle of this wasteland were two solitary desks, covered in layers of newspaper. A man's shape shuffled out from underneath and stood up.

'Dougie! How's it going?' asked Robert.

I knew it was definitely Robert because of his navy-and-magenta striped tie, although blotches of beige and ochre had blossomed on the silk.

'Fantastic. Great,' I said. 'Weren't there two of you here?'

'You'll be thinking of Alistair. I traded him,' said Robert.

'You traded him?'

'Just this morning, in fact. I got a good deal.'

'What for?'

I had meant why had he traded Alistair, but Robert had already darted underneath one of the desks. He emerged, holding a huge bird's head. I looked at it more closely and realised it was a leather mask with a massive beak.

'Where did you get this?' I asked.

Robert tapped the side of his nose and smiled. 'Just got it this morning.'

'What's it for?' I asked.

Robert bent forward and whispered, 'This recession, it's a plague. A pestilence has been visited upon us.'

'It's genuine?' I asked.

Robert nodded. 'They wore these to sniff out the foulness,' he continued, his eyes shining.

'Can I have a shot?' I asked.

Robert considered this for a moment. He was probably thinking about the bottles of Chablis, the lines of coke we had shared down in Corney & Barrow; I know I was. He nodded and, cradling it gently, stroked his grubby finger down the length of the beak before holding it out to me.

I put it over my head and tried to fasten the straps; my fingers were like swollen pork sausages. Then I felt Robert's cool fingers brush against mine, and he pulled the leather straps tight. The mask was heavy; it smelt of old leather and somehow of herbs. I turned to look at Robert. The glass eye-pieces blurred my sight, but I could see him clearly enough, nodding at me as if he had created me himself.

I jerked my head right back and, aiming straight for Robert's eye, launched the beak forward. He clutched his hands to his head and sank down onto his knees. He stayed there for a moment, as if in prayer, and then fell forward, the navy-and-magenta-and-beige-and-ochre tie spilling out to the side.

As I went down the stairs, I paused on the landing to wipe the blood from my beak with my sleeve. The heaviness of the mask felt right, the straps tight around the back of my head felt good. In the cold wintry sunlight, the beak cast a long shadow on the staircase wall.

Everything went quiet when I went into the office. People stopped typing, stopped speaking and slowly stood up. Elliot came out of his office.

'Who are you? Who sent you?' he said, backing away from me. 'Dougie, is that you? Dougie?'

I could hear the sweat in his voice.

Bed

by DAN SPENCER

I wake when Paul pulls off the sheet, saying, 'Up you get.'
He's standing in his underwear. It isn't usual for me that I've
slept naked. To teach him a lesson for waking me, I roll onto
my back and he says, 'No, I'm blind!', staggering out onto the
landing. I blink a little. The emulsion smells cool and still. The
sash windows (newly glossed) are open and the town is quiet. I
watch Paul's legs walking off.

The bed is about the last thing in the house, because, as I
told Paul, we were always going to need somewhere to sleep.
I knew not to paint myself into a corner. It's been the whole
summer. Paul arrived the day after he broke up at the school.
I was here before that because I'm between things at the
moment. We can't agree if we're going to sell or rent. It started
as a spring-clean but then all of a sudden we'd cleared everything out. Paul uses the word 'unfurnished' and I realise it was
his decision. When we repainted, I drove to buy supplies as if
it was my idea. It wasn't. Next we were pulling up the carpets.
'Minimalist,' Paul said. But I still don't know his plans. Some
days he talks about 'letting agents', other days 'auction'.

Valuables, we move into storage. We've made lots of trips to
the tip, or to the charity shops in town, but some of it we save
for resale. Occasionally, Paul and I need to discuss who should
have some or other 'item of personal value'. But if I'm on my
own and I find something I want, I pocket it. There are large,
important things – the cherry wardrobe, the china dinner
set – but unlike these, the brass bedstead has not, we believe,
retained its value.

It's a rickety old thing. A leg is bent and one of the bed
knobs is loose. Paul and I were always fighting in here because
it's the largest room in the house. Mostly it was for play but
that fight, when Paul collided with the bedstead, that had been
about a girl.

We mean to begin with the bed but then don't get to it until
the afternoon. It's a big house and you become caught up in
things. You get side-tracked by other small tasks which then
turn into big tasks. You intend to paint a wall but first you

want to remove the wallpaper or fill in every hole that you can find (and you can always find more holes). Other problems present themselves, with the plaster or the wiring or the foundations or whatever it is. Some days we don't see each other until the evening. We've spent the summer this way, working through the rooms unsystematically but steadily, and separately for the most part.

It's messy, physical work. Every day, I wear a rugby shirt of my father's, tucked unstylishly into an oversized pair of Dad's trousers, belted with his belt. I have the old clothes on for obvious reasons.

Early afternoon, Beth telephones to ask how we're getting on. I don't think she expected this to take so long. I tell her that Paul is probably somewhere and should I get him? She says no and to say she says hi. I'm positive today. Today maybe we'll finish. I explain to Beth about Paul's plan for the bed. 'Why carry it down to the front door?' he says. He says we can post the parts through the bedroom window and drop them from there onto the driveway below. Beth says it's typical of Paul to over-think.

Up in the bedroom, Paul has heaved the king mattress onto its side and leant it against a wall. The toolbox is out on the floorboards and Paul's looking at the bedframe, weighing in his hands a screwdriver and a spanner. He has lighter hair than mine. A narrow waist. A slim frame. Naturally it reminds me of my mother.

'For a couple of years I slept here a lot,' he says. 'I'd wake up at three or four in the morning and start worrying. I don't know about what. What do children worry about? Something happening to their parents, I expect. I couldn't sleep so I'd come to their room and get in at the bottom of the bed then manoeuvre up between them. Did you do that too? It's funny that we never met each other in here.'

I don't think of Mum and Dad in the bed. They're older, when I think of them. We're teenagers and they're out late.

They have friends. They have lives. But their bedroom door is closed and I'm on the landing. Paul and Beth are inside. The bed doesn't make a sound. This is before it got damaged. I can hear panting but I don't know whether it's Beth or Paul.

It disassembles straightforwardly, in the end. The slats go out the window easily, as do three long rails which seesaw on the sill before swinging downward. Then Paul takes a hammer to the head rail. It doesn't need doing. However mangled it becomes it's never going to fit the window. I'm at a loose end so I stand and watch him turning it into a piece of car wreckage. Paul's tired. It's been the whole summer, as I say. But he keeps hammering. Steady. Unsystematic. When he gives up he looks completely alone but how can I help him?

'I think we should hold onto the house for now,' he says.

'It makes sense,' I say. 'In this climate.'

As I carry the head rail down to the car, Paul lets the mattress thud on the floor. I collect the slats in the driveway. You can hear Paul showering. The bathroom windows are open. Open too is the door, and so are all the other windows of the house. I put everything into the car. The head rail is a giant, brass ribcage.

When I get back from the tip, I find Paul asleep in the bedroom. He's lying naked on the mattress, on his front, sleeping like he fell that way. I'm suddenly very tired too and as I lower my body beside his I'm already dreaming – my shoulder snug against Paul's hip – my head falling away – a hand resting on my chest – a hand, at rest, on his leg.

[CATEGORY D]

LUCIAN FREUD
Two Men, 1987–8
GMA 3410 · purchased 1988

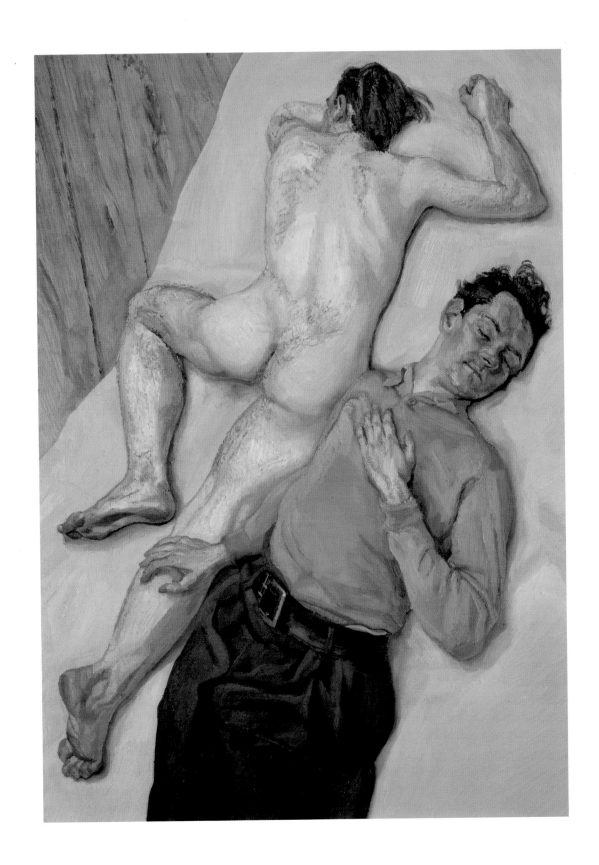

Echo

by STEPHI STACEY

The diagnosis was a label that I did not want to wear but could not remove. We tried everything - pulling, tearing, scratching, scraping – but it would not break. It just continued to break me.

1

I tried to remain calm while an army of doctors huddled around me and whispered words in a language that I didn't understand. I have yet to discover whether their cryptic terms were for my benefit – a misguided attempt to shield me from reality – or for theirs – to add to the illusion that they actually knew what they were doing.

All I know is this: the truth was lost when it hit the language barrier.

I could tell from their anxious tones that something was seriously wrong – I just didn't know what. They left me to fill in the blanks and of course, as anyone with any imagination will be aware: unknown monsters triple in size.

Everything is much more frightening in the dark.

Apparently doctors can only speak in plain English whilst in the presence of your parents. Otherwise they run the risk of being left alone to cope with the tears of someone else's child. That's not what all those years of medical training were for.

2

There were countless scans and examinations – each one giving the same verdict: terminal. People made promises that they knew couldn't be kept and I tried to believe every single one, even though my body was a walking, talking piece of evidence to the contrary.

I was happy to have my disease confined to a ward so long as I did not have to accompany it. I spat in the face of the nurse who told me that this wasn't an option. Then I cried.

They described me as a broken clock – the hands are moving forwards but they are not in time with everything else. I will fall apart.

3

Some people like sympathy, or – should I say – they like the benefits that come with it, the free-rides. Perhaps they like the way it changes their relationships with others; I do not. I want to be known for myself – not for my illness, not as 'the sick girl'.

Other people, *healthy* people, don't understand. They ask far too many questions – as if I actually want to talk about the thing that's killing me. Even more than before, the clichéd 'How are you?' is thrown into every conversation.

People never really want to know how you're feeling – they ask because convention dictates it and because they wish to give the impression that they care. We are taught the appropriate answer from childhood – 'I'm fine' – even though it's never completely true.

I think that we lie because the truth is too frightening, because we like to pretend that monsters don't exist.

The only problem is: they do.

4

There were times when I grew tired of the medication, when I lost track of the amount of time spent in hospital, when I wished for it to stop. Drugs numb the pain but they also numb emotion – suck out all the feeling until you don't know whether it's better to be yourself in pain or not yourself at all.

The most awful part is the space between: when you don't know what will break next, if the next crack will be permanent…

It's the fear – more than the pain – that tears you apart; it's not knowing what kind of monster is coming for you.

I try to capture my life in words because it's the only way I know how. These letters will remain while I cannot – they are the only mark I can make on a world where I have little time left.

I write this because I fear oblivion; because – if I can't live forever – I want to leave a part of me behind.

EDVARD MUNCH
The Sick Girl (Das kranke Mädchen), 1896
GMA 2309 · purchased 1981

Lily's Purple Heart

by JESSAMY COWIE

When I was younger I had a friend called Lily. Lily was the kind of person who seemed to fill a room with life. If she found something boring she would change that and turn even the dullest chores into adventures. She could make the doctor seem like an evil scientist intent on injecting you with deadly diseases or turn a maths lesson into a way for teachers to hypnotise children using coded numbers.

Lily died when I was nine. She had leukaemia. She knew all along. No-one at school did. When she missed school to go to the doctors she told us that it was because she had a 'purple heart' from eating too many purple Starbursts. She said the doctors had to make it the right colour again. I can't remember whether I believed her or not; she was always very good at adding believable twists just when people began to question her stories. When she took her pills at lunch she told us that the red ones would change her heart back to the right colour and the white ones would keep it from turning purple again.

I never told her but I was always jealous of her having a purple heart. It seemed to me that she got all the attention because of it. In secret I ate as many purple Starbursts as I could get my hands on and tried to persuade my mum to take me to the doctors. I was convinced that my heart, like Lily's, was gradually turning purple. When Lily went into hospital, me and my mum went to the Build a Bear factory and made her a special bear. Instead of the red hearts you can choose to put in, we put in a purple Starburst.

The bear was named Violet and became Lily's constant companion. She told me all about the conversations they had and all their secret midnight feasts on Lily's hospital bed. I wished more than ever that I could join in with their games. To me Lily's life seemed almost perfect. She had a television at the end of her bed, other children living in the next room and piles of get-well presents. I didn't notice how thin she was or that she was all alone in her little room. It didn't matter to me that she had to be helped to walk or that the television didn't work. I saw only the things I wanted to and I was green with envy.

About a week before she died I went to see her again. I left my mum in the waiting area to talk to Lily's mother and went to find Lily. As I opened the door I stopped in confusion. She was fast asleep, just a gaunt pale face hidden in a single bed that swamped her frame. I hardly recognised her. For the first time in weeks I truly saw her. In that moment my jealousy evaporated. I hated the silence of the room and the bare walls. I wanted to run as fast as I could back to my mum in the waiting room and drive home. The truth terrified me and I wanted so badly to leave it behind. Shaking, I placed the card I had made for her on the bedside table and backed towards the door holding back a sob. I glanced for one last time at the unfamiliar face and closed the door behind me.

In the weeks that followed her death I didn't talk much to anyone. I couldn't accept that I wouldn't see her again and I was haunted by the memory of her face the last time I saw her, but as the last few visits faded from my mind I began to remember Lily differently. I remembered how magical she was at storytelling and how she could make you believe anything she wanted you to. When I think of her like this I can't help smiling because I know that every time someone plays a prank or makes up elaborate lies, Lily will be somewhere, laughing along with the joke.

[CATEGORY B]

EDVARD MUNCH
Detail from *The Sick Girl* (*Das kranke Mädchen*), 1896
GMA 2309 · purchased 1981

Sabine, 2000

by JOSIE ROGERS

Oh, cover me –
she sighs as she rolls over
all skin
milky, hot, bed-scented

She turns and tugs and settles
like an oak stirring in a gale
The sheet billows, sinking, swaddling
– a swell of second skin
With caution it lands
and puckers

Like a cleft of warm flesh
or the fold of a page of a book
or the withering of a leaf

Or the crease of the skin of her arm
when we're older.

[CATEGORY C]

ALISON WATT
Sabine, 2000
GMA 4353 · purchased
(Knapping Fund) 2001

How it Goes

by IAIN MATHESON

You know how it goes; in a glossy
magazine a picture of something
or other, you spot some detail in
the background, let's say a bell, the old-
fashioned kind schools once had, and you're off
wondering how it would sound, how you'd
describe that sound to anyone who
asked (a clown, a bureaucrat), without
falling back on the usual tired
repertoire of dings and bongs. You're well
aware that the clown might in fact be
a ghost, having passed away in a
big top mishap when his circus was
touring a small town in Italy
in which you happen to know that a
famous film-star was born, her mother
(legend says) perfected a secret
recipe for pesto, the kind you
can now buy in any superstore
where shelves are listlessly stacked by the
would-be paramour of Denise the
checkout girl who works overnight shifts
(a student of psychology, she
plans to document what people buy
at 3 a.m. and why); her dog is
not allowed in the shop and must be
left at home where one night it raised the
alarm and almost saved the life of
an old man fallen asleep with a
lighted cigarette for company –
ironically a man who had
been in his own day a saviour of
dogs via the nearby animal
rescue centre, now demolished and
rebuilt as a pub, the landlord swears
his parents are aliens, a claim
so unlikely that even local
conspiracy theorists, who pride
themselves on openness to extra-
terrestrial phenomena, are
hard-pressed to suspend their disbelief.

[CATEGORY E]

Come Rain or Shine

by ELEANOR YOUNG

Fog lay thick upon the city, and the rain fell in heavy sheets upon the tarmac. Ants scurried quickly away from anywhere that came under siege, a place where droplets fell so thick and fast that no insect could ever hope to survive. Rain fell on the heads of the office workers that walked slowly by, and the umbrellas on the street formed an unyielding wall of grey. Shiny shoes sloshed in the gutter, which was only occupied by the unlucky few who were running late for their meeting. A taxi sped quickly by, and an old man who had borne the brunt of the water it had thrown up shook his fist angrily at its disappearing behind.

The wind howled, merciless, around the art gallery, deserted except for the few Chinese tourists that wondered around the grounds, sheltered underneath their throwaway waterproof ponchos. The grass lay sodden upon the wet earth, and the men that had come to cut it earlier that day had been sent away by a grumpy grounds man. In a little-visited corner of the grounds, two white blocks lay, a sculpture left outside to face the Scottish weather.

Two mothers walked by it, followed, like baby ducks, by their small fleet of children – six in all. Expensive coats bundled up to just under their chin, they minced their way carefully over the squelching ground towards a park bench. Their offspring, on the contrary, stamped their small feet down in any muddy puddles they could find. Their little welly boots provided little defence against the dirty water, but the rosy glow in their cheeks showed to what extent they were enjoying their day.

'We claim this fort,' yelled a little boy as he and his two friends quickly dived behind one of two white blocks. This left the three girls to crouch uncomfortably on the flagstones. The two older girls turned to face each other, and were soon engaged in deep conversation. The youngest of the three – clad in a pink, Hello Kitty raincoat – could not sit still. She ran her small fingers over the bumpy, painted bronze, at the edge of the sculpture, and even through her gloves she could feel the coldness of the metal.

The water cascaded over the edge of the blocks where they sat, and a small ant weaved its way slowly across the flagstones at their feet, dodging the heavy drops of water that fell upon the earth.

The little girl's eyes tracked its movement, slowly, carefully, like a hunter following its prey. Inside her tiny head, cogs whirled, imagining a world in which she was a small as an ant. How big this piece of art would be! Mountains, and valleys, which flooded with the pitter patter of water. The world would be so dangerous, so deadly, yet it would consist of only the pure whiteness of these blocks. Imagine it in winter when the frost came! She could hide silently whilst she watched the progress of it across the smooth white surface. Her tiny feet could glide across the white, smooth surface, where the frost was invisible. So cold would it be, but the ice upon the surface of the block would be invisible.

In the spring, the sun would shine for the first time upon the blocks, upon a sparkling, clean surface, because the mud that was kicked up last autumn was halted so fiercely by the cold.

Oh! And think of the summer! She could lie on the top of one of the blocks, cradled softly, safely there. Maybe she could turn her face towards the light, like a sunflower. When the leaves fell gently off the trees in autumn, she would venture dangerously across the flat land, like a climber crossing a boulder field. Huge spaces would open up above her head, and occasionally, she would have to squeeze through a gap so small her whole body would tremble at the effort.

Fog lay thick upon the art gallery. The rain came down unceasingly, and in a little-visited corner of the grounds a small party hurried away. Two girls followed closely behind their mothers, and behind came three boys, faces painted brown with mud. At the back, a little girl in a pink, Hello Kitty raincoat was trying hard to keep up. Every three steps her small head would turn back, her brown eyes focused

upon the work of art they had just left. Into the café trailed
the small group. The last person of all through the door was
a little girl in a pink, Hello Kitty raincoat. She let the hefty
door bang heavily upon the backs of her knees, and, with
one last look around, went inside.

On the street outside shiny shoes trampled down on the
pavement, and the roaring gutter was only graced by the
small, unlucky few that happened to be running late for
their meeting that day. The many dark umbrellas formed an
unyielding wall of grey.

RACHEL WHITEREAD
Untitled (Pair), 1999
GMA 4367 · purchased with the
assistance of the Art Fund 2001

Snow

by IAN MCDONOUGH

That winter there was nothing in our minds but snow.
    We dreamed of overhangs, cornices,
    avalanches, drifts.

The sun, barely as high as a March Hare's leap
    hung like a faded orange kiss. Trees stood
    naked and appalled in fields.

Ice-clad, the phone lines failed to bring relief –
    we fed on histories, gorged on myths,
    submarined to inner worlds.

Snared in shadow, the frozen village craved fresh light
    while, locked inside our whitened lives
    we heaved like earthquakes.

[CATEGORY E]

JOAN EARDLEY
Catterline in Winter, 1963
GMA 888 · purchased 1964

One for Sorrow

by JOE STEEL

Her hands are cold. Entwined with mine, they seem old. Older. The back spidered with blue, palms lined with folds. Comforted by the rhythm of her breathing, I lean back against the soft silk. The raindrops hammer against glass, the hubbub of night-time traffic is a far-away sound. Orange streetlight spills into the room from a gap in the curtains. I watch it shimmer on the carpet, as droplets dance down the pane, endlessly merging and separating; glass pearls, beautiful, fragile. She murmurs in her sleep. Escape. She seeks escape. With the base of my thumb, I stroke her hand. I bring across my other, holding her fingers tightly, squeezing, to let her know I'm here. Silently I pull it closer, towards my chin, nesting it there. A pulse beats, the rain drums. I move my hand upwards, placing her knuckles against my lips. A kiss. Returning her arm to its original position, I look down at her, turning my head. Her face, full of impish glee and untainted purity once upon a time, now veiled by age. Wrinkles, like scars across her face; a mouth which droops at the corners; a brow furrowed by time. Grey hair, now thinning, frames her face with sliver curls. A crown of ivory. I survey our kingdom. Quaint. Two smiling faces gaze back at me. Framed, blessed. I look to the dresser. Two sets of false teeth. Two pairs of glasses. Two pairs of shoes. Smiling, I breathe out, sighing.

In the kitchen, I'm alone with my thoughts. Silently, I rinse and dry one of the crystal tumblers, replacing it in its home cupboard. Returning to my starting position before the sink, I look out the window: watching, contemplating. In the semi-darkness, colour slowly seeping from the horizon, the glass changes: a moment of reflection, a moment of clarity. The boiler hums, the radiator whines. Through my darkened silhouette, the garden is peaceful. From over the fence, a lone blackbird floats down on to the grass. Precise in his movements, he hops around the garden, searching for worms, to and fro. I look up. The clouds are leaving. Behind them, countless diamonds shimmer on their dark background. High above, the moon is suspended. Hung by an invisible tether. The crowning jewel. Hauntingly beautiful. A single note steals me from my imaginings. Back in the garden, my little friend has been joined by a female counterpart. Looking at each other inquisitively, they appear to be conversing. Catching up. Exchanging stories. One ebony, one mahogany. Leaping across the garden, they twist and waltz, dancing. Dancing. I watch them, transfixed. Without warning, the dance ends. The music stops. Their tones are harsher, more shrill. And then they are gone. I breathe out, puzzled by their sudden exit. I notice something out the corner of my eye. With a flourish of inky feathers, a solitary magpie now stands in the centre of the garden. Sinister and threatening. It cocks its head. Out of its long, sharp beak, an unwelcome noise tolls. One for sorrow. Instinctively, I feel tense. As I'm tying my dressing gown tighter, I hear noise from the bedroom. A shout. A call for help. Against the protests from my knee, I rush through. I stop in the doorway. Looking at the bed, all I see is a mess of sheets. A single hand appears on the opposite side of the covers. I tear round. She's there: crumpled and confused. Trying to get up; a look of frustration flashes across her face. Unable to watch her struggle, I bend down, taking hold of her arm. Sensing discomfort, I only get her as far as a sitting position. Together, we sit against the bed, my arm around her shoulders. A sign of safety. A sign of protection. I listen to her talk. About her dream. Her nightmare. I grasp her hand. With my other, I brush the matted hair from her face. Looking up, I notice her pills on the bedside table. A glass of water. Discarded Alzheimer's medication. Prescribed, but discarded. I respected her decision. Brushing away the tablets, I take one of the books from the table. Rossetti's poems. I open it at the page bookmarked. We must not look at goblin men. She nestles her head on my shoulder. We must not buy their fruit. Who knows upon what soil they fed their hungry, thirsty roots.

A cold mist clings stubbornly to the dewy ground. The grass glitters in the morning air. The sky before me is splashed with colour. A fiery orange radiates from the skyline, changing to pinks and indigos. The ominous silhouettes of rectangular obelisks project upwards, threatening in their brutality. Nearby, the woods mirror the demeanour of the tower blocks: ominous, threatening. I listen to the welcome silence of the morning, only interrupted by the gentle calls of the birds. The rhythm of my steps echo around the street. Arm pressed tightly to my side, morning newspaper protected, I fish for my keys in my jacket pocket. Hearing the click of the lock, I cross the threshold. The sound of radio static meets my ears. Curious, I wander down the hall. From through the kitchen door, the linoleum glistens. The floor is soaking. Overflowing, the sink sits smugly in the middle of the worktop. I tiptoe across the water. Arm deep, I remove the plug and turn off the taps. Drying my hands, I end the incessant crackling. Through the open back door, I hear sounds of a struggle. Still in her nightie, now blackened by soil, she digs through the bare flowerbed, searching. Searching. Her engagement ring. Her hands coated in earth. Remember. I remember. Lost and found several years ago, probably now sitting on her bedside table, the scene before me has become common in the last few months. Loss. Nightmares. Forgetting. I loathed seeing her distressed. Vulnerable. I lead her inside. Help her get cleaned up. Trembling. Shaking.

Inside, she looks tired. Eyes, coloured by lack of sleep. Eyelids heavy. My heart aches. She asks for him. Our son. She looks around: anxious, waiting. Fighting back tears, I tell her that he no longer lives with us. Confused. She leaves the room. Alone, I sip my tea, watching the steam rise higher and higher. Delicately. Higher and higher. Standing at the sink, mug washed, I look out of the window. A moment of reflection. A moment of clarity. The magpie has returned. Menacing. Solitary. I turn away.

The bedside clock ticks calmly. She is sitting on the bed, asleep. Her eyes are swollen. Red. She's been crying. I lean across, pressing my lips against her forehead. Lingering. Remember. Her hands are cold.

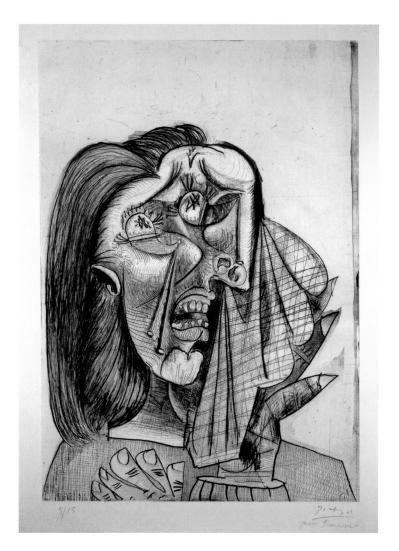

PABLO PICASSO

Weeping Woman (La Femme qui pleure), 1937

GMA 4774 · accepted by H.M. Government in lieu of Inheritance Tax on the Estate of Joanna Drew and allocated by H.M. Government to the Scottish National Gallery of Modern Art 2005

The Woman Speaks

by MOLLY-MAY ALLAN

Let the curse be lifted,
Please let it rise, oh please.
Slaughter my pig nose,
Demolish my stone-age teeth,
Burn my chopstick cheeks.
Darken my starry eyes,
Stab my dragon hand,
Bleach my knitted hair.
Catch my fish gills neck,
Let my beautiful spirit be released.
For I am beautiful inside.

[CATEGORY B]

PABLO PICASSO

Detail from *Weeping Woman* (*La Femme qui pleure*), 1937

GMA 4774 · accepted by H.M. Government in lieu of Inheritance Tax on
the Estate of Joanna Drew and allocated by H.M. Government to the
Scottish National Gallery of Modern Art 2005

The Girl in the Window

by EILIDH MACKINNON

When Scott sees a pair of raised eyebrows through the window opposite him, he nearly knocks himself out on the desk by falling on it.

There's a weighted silence, and then: 'Wow. Did you just die? It'd be a cool story for me to tell but kind of awkward if you died, because I'm pretty sure I'd have to report it to the police that you did that weird flailing thing and then collapsed, and that's not really the sort of thing you'd want on your gravestone—'

'I'm not dead,' Scott protests from the floor, where he's been lying for a few seconds, partly due to pain but mostly out of the sheer embarrassment that's going to accompany getting up and facing whoever it is in the house next door. His voice gets caught in his sleeve as he says it, but he thinks it got the point across.

He eases himself to his feet, gripping onto the desk for support as he does, and forces himself not to wince. That'll be another bruise to add to his growing collection.

Through their open windows, the girl is grinning. Her hair is short, loose dark brown curls tucked behind her ears and straight thick dark eyebrows sitting above her mischievous hazel eyes. Dark freckles are erratically dotted across her face but move with her cheeks as a smile pulls up at her lips.

She's maybe a year younger than Scott – twelve, maybe – but she looks tiny, dwarfed in her purple t-shirt, her collarbone very defined and bare. Scott shuffles self-consciously, wrapping a curtain across his chest trying to hide more of his substantial bulk.

'Good. Great. Graceful, by the way,' the girl grins teasingly. 'The fall, I mean. Did I scare you?'

'No, I just—'

'Because I've been reliably informed I make people walk into walls. Or in your case, vertically and face first into a desk, but I'll take what I can get.'

Scott doesn't know quite what to say to that, and as he pauses, the girl's smile falters somewhat.

'You didn't scare me,' Scott stutters finally. 'You—' he clears his throat and tugs his window up for ease of communication, letting his makeshift curtain-toga slip slightly to reveal part of his t-shirt underneath. 'I wasn't expecting anyone to be watching me.'

The girl frowns. 'I wasn't *watching* you. I was just – glancing. Momentarily.'

'It looked a lot like staring.'

'How would you know? You only saw me for a second and then—'. The girl makes a motion with her hand, tipping over, and adds an explosion sound out of the corner of her mouth. 'Again, graceful. Very impressive.'

'Thanks,' Scott says, inflecting the word with sarcasm, but it comes out less biting than he intends.

Her eyes are flicking around taking in his surroundings and Scott can feel himself coming out in a cold sweat under the girl's unflinching gaze. Her eyes roll to a stop and her mouth quirks up, 'You like Belle and Sebastian too?'

This confuses Scott for a second, the question coming out of the blue but he nods, 'Yes, I do like them; my Dad took me to one of their concerts last year and…' He leaves his sentence hanging in the air as he looks down, finally relinquishing his hold on the curtain to stare at the t-shirt stretched over his stomach: '…he bought me a t-shirt.'

The girl nods thoughtfully, the glint of a gold stud in her left ear catching the light of the sun. Scott notes that her right ear is bare of any such adornment, perhaps a fashion statement. He doesn't really know enough girls to be able to tell if it is a common look. Her hands come up to shove deep into her pockets. 'You lived here long?'

'As long as I can remember.'

'Yeah, yesterday,' the girl says. 'Me, I mean. Moving. Here. Yesterday.'

Scott bites down the urge to laugh at how fumbling she sounds because the girl's shoulders are tight; he thinks she'll take it personally. 'You're new?'

Thinking on it Scott had seen the vans outside and heard people talking but hadn't paid much attention to it. He'd just picked up the newest edition of his favourite comic and that had absorbed his attention for the day. He hadn't considered people would move into the house next-door so quickly. It felt like the shouting couple with the wailing baby had only just moved out. And what a relief that had been.

'Yeah.' The girl takes a quick breath, her chest rising, and it looks like she's about to say something else before Scott interrupts.

'I'm Scott,' he says, and holds his hand out, because if there's one thing his mother taught him, it's manners.

A few seconds pass, and it's not until the girl starts laughing before Scott realises that there's three meters of empty air and a two storey drop between them. He flushes, and pulls his hand back to his side. 'I. Um.'

'No, it's fine,' the girl says, and her smile seems more genuine than the one she had been pulling before, even though she's trying to tamp it down. She steps out onto her window ledge with a clumsy elegance and perches, like a little bird, on the small platform jutting out from her window. 'I'm Cora.'

'Nice to meet you,' Scott says automatically, still feeling his blush at the back of his neck and down the collar of his shirt.

Cora nods again, shoving a hand back in her pocket; the other firmly grips the window ledge, but Scott can see her fingers moving in her pocket, like she's fiddling nervously with something.

'Yeah,' Cora says, and there it is: the uncertain, tiny tick of a smile on Cora's face, like she doesn't know what to make out of him yet. 'You too.'

[CATEGORY C]

GEORGES ROUAULT
*Head, c.*1935–40
GMA 968 · presented by Sir Alexander Maitland in memory of his wife Rosalind 1960

Minotaur Slayer

by IAN MCDONOUGH

All through the baking days
he stands to serve coffee and beers,
the fat boy from Platanés.

He dreams of saving these sepulchral Northern girls
from the Minotaur's sulphurous, foetid breath,
of splicing open its filthy, bestial gut
with a sword that glints like polished ice.

All the small change they tossed so carelessly
into a chipped green ashtray on the bar
he trousered, week on week, season upon season,
watching, in the course of fifteen baking years,
it grow and grow into a venerable hoard.

Soon, but never quite today, he'll go and buy
that icy, shining sword. Only now,
as he clomps around the hotel bar
upon these shiny flint-edged hooves,
he wonders just whose gut it is that he should pierce.

[CATEGORY E]

PABLO PICASSO
The Death of a Monster (La Fin d'un monstre), 1937
GMA 3891 · purchased with the support of the Heritage Lottery Fund and
the Art Fund 1995

September Storm

by MICHELLE WARDS

We lie in the grass and stare at the sky. The fog obscures the moon's light and I think it's going to rain but I don't say anything to Anne. Storms and darkness don't scare her like they do me. My sleep is haunted by nightmares of shadows and floods. What does she dream of? Can you have nightmares if you're not scared of anything?

I wait on her to break our silence. The grass rustles in the autumn breeze. Dusk weaves in amongst the weeds, calling me back home. She reaches her hand out to touch mine. I can feel her bones trying to escape through the skin.

'At least I'll never have to put up with another freezing winter,' she says. Anne worships the sunshine, running outside at the faintest hint of summer. I always have to hide my skin from the burn of the rays.

'Don't say that.'

'Lighten up! It's not you that's ill.'

She throws a handful of grass in my face.

'Hey!' I say, grabbing some from the ground and scattering it in her hair. I want to laugh but it makes me feel guilty.

'Let's make the longest daisy chain of all time,' she says, getting up and dusting off the mess from her skirt. The flowers are dotted among the overgrown grass and soon we have a pile big enough to start threading together. Anne wraps the chain around her neck and sits down on the ground beside the cliff edge.

'Don't get too close,' I say.

'It's beautiful down here,' she shouts.

'Really?'

'Come look.'

I go over and sit down, letting my legs dangle down into the abyss. There's nothing much to see except the whites of the waves and a light from a ship in the distance.

'One day this piece of land will erode, fall down the cliff and into the water,' she says.

'That's scary,' I reply, edging backwards.

'Nothing we can do to stop it.'

'So sad,' I say but she just shrugs.

'Maybe I should just jump now. Get it over with.'

'Not funny,' I say and my eyes water.

'Don't get upset. I'm only kidding. I'm going to get bald first just like the rest of them.'

'I don't know how you can joke about it.'

'Sorry. I'm just weird I guess.'

She stares off into the distance. From her face you'd never know a disease is devouring her insides. She begins to pick the heads off the flowers and scatters them into the sea below.

Lightning cracks the sky open as we walk back across the field. We spin round and round with our hands dancing in the rain. The cold pierces my face and the dizziness forces us to sit down.

'They'll be looking for us soon.' I try to pull Anne up from the ground but she won't budge.

'Can't go any further. I'll stay for the storm.'

'It's dangerous.'

'Nothing can hurt me now.'

'We should go home.'

'Live a little. This might be my last storm ever. I want to remember it.'

'You live in Scotland! There's a new storm every ten minutes! Even if you died tomorrow this wouldn't be your last.'

We both laugh even though I said the 'd' word. Her hand shivers in mine.

'I will stay for five minutes and then we have to go,' I say but she knows I'll wait as long as she wants.

I take off my coat and wrap it around her. The storm-filled clouds howl. We lie there until the world turns black and a river of rain begins to flow. I daydream of a sun that makes the grass around us grow and grow and grow until we are buried so deep that nothing and no one will ever be able to find us.

[CATEGORY D]

JOAN EARDLEY
Seeded Grasses and Daisies, September, 1960
GMA 889 · purchased with funds given by an anonymous donor 1964

Oban

by JANE BONNYMAN

In come the fishing boats,
holding memory like the day's catch –
the silver flickers of life slowed by air.
The first to reach the harbour
beneath you now, as you stand,
one elbow resting on the railing;

into its blue shadow you stare
and see Ganavan, the evening
when the sun chose this curve of bay
to turn golden, make Mediterranean.
You bend to collect mussel shells
to take home, spread on the kitchen table.

Mother says you might find a pearl,
but you don't believe her
until the moment a tiny stone
rolls between your finger and thumb.
You thought it was forgotten,
how you pressed it in her palm
and how she smiled then –
That's one. That's one.

[CATEGORY E]

SIR JAMES GUTHRIE
Oban, 1893
NG 2087 · purchased 1947

The Procedure

by OLGA WOJTAS

Beau talks. Beau talks and talks. He talks about how the war in Afghanistan differs from the Vietnam War. He talks about the European banking system. He talks about the time JFK came to dinner. He talks about the Apollo programme.

But people seem increasingly unwilling to listen. He opines that this is less to do with what he says than how he looks.

'In the past, age was valued for its wisdom,' he says. 'Now it's despised for its wrinkles. I think I should have some work done.'

Leah tells him how distinguished he looks, and mentions Walter Cronkite and Alistair Cooke. Deceased, says Beau. He produces a brochure for a new clinic whose deal includes tightening the vocal cords to recreate a youthful voice.

Beau talks about JFK's voice, about Khrushchev's voice, about Khrushchev hammering the UN desk with his shoe. He talks about the Bay of Pigs and the Cuban missile crisis. Leah listens and nods and rings the clinic to make an appointment, as she is instructed.

The clinic is as plush as the Waldorf-Astoria and Dr Catalano's voice is strong and youthful. He takes photographs of Beau, full face and profile, and then, through computer-aided design, indicates what his surgeon's art can achieve.

Beau talks about Harvard Medical School, about the Mayo Clinic, about the American Holistic Medical Association. He talks about Dr Martin Luther King and Dr Condoleezza Rice. Dr Catalano smiles and gets him to sign a number of forms.

A week later, Leah brings Beau in for the procedure. She kisses him goodbye. Beau talks about Philip Marlowe and Moose Malloy.

Leah makes her way to the Tea Box Cafe in Takashimaya on Fifth Avenue and has some Japanese sandwiches and a rose tea. Beau's voice is in her head, talking about the tea ceremony and Madame Butterfly and the Fukushima nuclear power plant.

When she sets off to do some shopping on Fifth Avenue, the voice continues: John D. Rockefeller and the Standard Oil Company; Martha Graham at the opening of the Radio City Music Hall; the memorial mass for William F. Buckley Jr in St Patrick's Cathedral.

Eventually, her cell-phone rings and she returns to the clinic. A charming young woman meets her at the entrance, and Leah can see that her brow would wrinkle if it could. Something has gone wrong. Dr Catalano's strong, youthful voice is higher and louder than before. The procedure has been a categorical success, he says. But for some reason which they cannot yet quite understand, Beau seems unable to talk.

Leah hurries to Beau's room. His face is still bandaged, but she can see a bloodshot glare.

'Beau, honey?' she says.

Beau grabs her purse, finds her diary and a pen, and writes in block capitals: 'SUE THE BASTARDS'.

Hiram Ginsberg may not look as young as Dr Catalano but he sounds just as reassuring. Something has clearly gone wrong. Perhaps Beau has suffered some sort of allergic reaction. Perhaps Dr Catalano has egregiously put filler in his vocal cords. They have a very good case.

Hiram Ginsberg knows this is not true. The clinic has been careful to get Beau to sign forms to the effect that whatever happens, he has no come-back. But Hiram makes his money from clients throwing good money after bad. And he talks a good game.

Even the judge acknowledges this, which Hiram hopes will be a comfort to Leah and Beau. But, says the judge, words are not enough and with regret, he must dismiss the plaintiff's case.

Beau, whose unlined face looks marvellous atop his stooped body, scribbles furiously. Hiram thanks the judge and indicates to Beau that it is all over. He waits for Leah to collect Beau and then realises she is no longer in court.

Leah is strolling in Central Park, listening to the pleasant rumble of the nearby traffic.

[CATEGORY D]

CHARLES HARVEY WEIGALL

Illustration to Burns's Song 'John Anderson, My Jo'

Self-Portrait
Oil on Canvas
53cm × 43cm

by SIMON WELLER

… heard a slow chant in a cave
And, peering over a rock, espied high priests
In clouds of incense, wonderfully robed, or

Making another desert journey, this
Merchant of light, arrested by an angel
Fell to his knees, piously raising his hands. Now

Mist rises continually from the canal.
The narrow stair seems ever steeper,
The floor unswept, the fire cold, unmade. Still

Light, delicious, strange as manna
Falls from the studio window overhead,
High above the temple, to the left, and

Brushes the surface of his pigment cheek. Clearly
Much remains to be done. The steady glance
Searches the mirror-glass, considering surface and form.

[CATEGORY E]

REMBRANDT VAN RIJN
Self-Portrait, aged 51, c.1657
NGL 072.46 · Edinburgh, Scottish National Gallery
(Bridgewater Loan, 1945)

Index